CONTENTS

In this book we are introduced to the Fenton family. We will meet Mr and Mrs Fenton, their children Laura and Daniel, and Laura and Daniel's grandparents Sally and Frank. Compare the high street of today with the high street of fifty years ago.

Laura Fenton is looking at computer games.

Laura has a brother called Daniel. He likes computer games too. Last time Laura was here, she spent her birthday money on a battery-powered toy dog that does somersaults.

FIFTY YEARS AGO

In the High Street

Karen Bryant-Mole

WAYLAND

Titles in the series
At Home
Going on a Trip
Having Fun
In the High Street

find Wayland on the Internet at http://www.wayland.co.uk

All Wayland books encourage children to read and help them improve their literacy.

 The contents page, page numbers, headings and index help locate specific pieces of information.

 The glossary reinforces alphabetic knowledge and extends vocabulary.

 The further information section suggests other books dealing with the same subject.

 Find out more about how this book is specifically relevant to the National Literacy Strategy on page 31.

Editor: Kim Protheroe
Consultant: Norah Granger
Cover design: White Design
Inside design: Michael Leaman
Picture glossary illustrator: John Yates
Photo stylist: Gina Brown
Production controller: Carol Titchener

First published in 1999 by
Wayland Publishers Limited
61 Western Road, Hove
East Sussex BN3 1JD

© Copyright 1999 Wayland Publishers Limited

Typeset in England by
Michael Leaman Design Partnership
Printed and bound in Italy by
L.G. Canale & C.S.p.A, Turin

British Library in Cataloguing Data
Bryant-Mole, Karen
    In the High Street. – (Fifty years ago)
    1. Shopping – History – Juvenile literature.
    2. Stores, Retail – History – Juvenile literature.
    I. Title 381.1'09

ISBN 0 7502 2306 5

Picture acknowledgements
The publishers would like to thank
the following for allowing their pictures
to be used in this book: Hulton Getty Cover;
Family Life Picture Library/Angela Hampton
Cover inset; Topham Picturepoint 7, 11, 13, 17,
21, 23, 25; Hulton Getty 5, 9, 15, 27; Mary Evans
19. All other pictures by Family Life Picture
Library/Angela Hampton.

These children liked the teddy and the lorry in the toy shop.

Fifty years ago teddies were usually stuffed with wood shavings and sawdust. Toy lorries and other vehicles looked like the vehicles that children would have seen on the roads.

I remember...

Sally Fenton is Laura and Daniel's granny. Her favourite toy was a doll. 'My doll was beautiful. She had eyes that opened and closed. I thought that was wonderful. Today, it seems that dolls have to be able to walk, talk and roller blade before children are impressed!'

BARBER

Daniel wants his hair cut so that he looks like his favourite pop star.

Daniel and his friends all like to have their hair cut in the same way. Last year they all had their hair cut in a different way. Daniel's mum wonders who he will want to look like next!

FIFTY YEARS AGO

This young man wanted the same hairstyle as a famous film star.

Just like today, people fifty years ago wanted to look fashionable. Going to the cinema was a very popular pastime and people wanted to look like the stars they saw on the screen.

I remember...

Frank Fenton is Laura and Daniel's grandpa. Frank's elder brother used to put a special cream called Brylcreem in his hair, to make it shiny and keep it in place. 'I used to think he looked so smart. But my mum just laughed and called him and his mates the Brylcreem Boys.'

BANK

Mrs Fenton is using her cash card to get money from a cash machine.

The cash machine is in the wall of her bank. She can get money from her bank account, even when the bank is closed. A computer works out how much money she has in her bank account.

This man went into the bank to take out his money.

When people buy goods today they often pay by credit card. Fifty years ago they could only pay with cash or write out a cheque.

I remember...

Sally Fenton's dad didn't have a bank account. 'My dad said he didn't trust banks with his money. He was paid his wages in cash every week. Of course, he was paid in old money, you know, pounds, shillings and pence. At school I wasn't very good at adding up. I found it very difficult. I'd never have been any good at working in a bank!'

Mr Fenton is deciding what to buy for dinner.

Today there are many different kinds of meat to buy. There are joints for roasting, chunks for stewing and slices for grilling. There are also lots of other meat products to choose from, such as kebabs and burgers.

This woman had to choose what to buy with her family's meat ration.

Food was rationed during the Second World War. Even after the war had ended, some foods were still hard to find. People had ration books and were only allowed to buy a small amount of meat each week.

I remember...

Frank Fenton remembers his local butcher's shop. 'The thing I remember most is the smell. And I remember the sawdust on the floor, too. The butcher chopped the meat with a huge knife and then you went over to a little office with a window where you gave your money to the butcher's wife.'

CLOTHES SHOP

Laura, her mum and her granny are shopping for some new clothes.

Laura likes wearing trousers. Her mum prefers skirts. Today, people can wear the clothes they like best. There are plenty of designs to choose from.

These women were buying Utility coats.

During and after the Second World War, material was in short supply. There was a scheme called the Utility Scheme. Manufacturers had to make very plain styles of clothes that did not waste any material.

I remember...

Sally Fenton's auntie hated Utility clothes. 'She didn't like the dull colours and styles. Then a new style came over from France, called the New Look. The dresses had narrow waists and long, full skirts. Clothes were still rationed in England but my auntie made a New Look dress from a pair of curtains!'

Mrs Fenton has bought some French bread for lunch.

Today, we can buy all kinds of bread. The most popular sort of bread is baked in factories, then sliced and put into plastic bags. People buy bread from supermarkets, corner shops and even petrol stations, as well as from the baker's.

All the cakes and bread in this baker's were baked in the shop.

There were small bakers' shops in towns and villages all around the country. Many bakers delivered fresh bread to their customers' homes every day. Today, many of these small shops have closed down.

I remember...

Sally Fenton remembers her dad being really fed up the year after the war ended. 'It had been a terrible winter and there wasn't enough wheat, so bread had to be rationed. My dad said it was bad enough putting up with rationing during the war, without it going on after the war finished.'

POST OFFICE

Mr Fenton is posting a package to his brother in Australia.

Mr Fenton is going to put the package on the electronic scales. The scales show how much it weighs and how much it will cost to send the package to Australia by air mail.

This man bought his stamps at the Post Office.

Instead of using electronic scales to weigh letters, the post office worker had to use a balance scale. He put the letter on the tray and used different weights until it balanced.

I remember...

When Frank Fenton was young, his family didn't have a phone at home. 'If we needed to get an urgent message to someone, we could use a public phone box. Or we could go down to the Post Office and send a telegram. If the message wasn't too urgent, we wrote a letter.'

Laura and Daniel enjoy the books and tapes they find in the library.

The Fentons can borrow all sorts of books from the library. Laura likes story books. Daniel often borrows books for school. The Fentons can borrow story tapes, music tapes, CDs and videos from their library, too.

These children sat at a big table to read their books.

Lots of the books that these children liked are still being enjoyed by children today. The tales of Mary Poppins and Winnie the Pooh were all on the bookshelves fifty years ago.

I remember...

Frank Fenton's mum took him to the library every Saturday. 'I liked choosing books from the library but the building itself looked a bit unfriendly. The librarian wasn't very fond of children. We all had to whisper and she told us off if we forgot.'

SUPERMARKET

The Fentons go to the supermarket once a week.

There are many kinds of foods to choose from. By the time the Fentons get to the checkout, their trolley will be piled high with shopping. When they get back home, they will put some of the food into the freezer.

This woman went shopping every day.

Fifty years ago, not many people had fridges. It was difficult to keep food fresh, so many people went to the shops every day. Self-service shops, like the one in the photograph, were a new idea.

I remember...

Sally Fenton's gran didn't like the new self-service shops at all. 'My gran complained because she had to walk around the shop, carrying everything herself. She liked going into the old-fashioned shops, where she could sit down on a chair and have a chat with the shopkeeper while he weighed out and wrapped up all the things on her shopping list.'

Daniel and his dad are having lunch at a fast food restaurant.

Daniel has a milk shake. His dad has a fizzy drink. Daniel likes going to fast food restaurants. They sell the sort of food and drinks he likes and people get served quickly.

These people were served by a waitress.

This photograph was taken in a Lyons' Corner House. Lyons' Corner Houses were very popular fifty years ago. As well as having tea in the cafe, the customers could also buy bread and cakes to take away.

I remember...

Sally Fenton remembers going to a Corner House with her parents and her sister for a birthday treat. 'It was very posh. There was music playing. The waitresses were friendly and polite. Mum said I could have whatever I liked, and I ordered a slice of cake.'

Mrs Fenton is buying some strawberries.

Strawberries are only grown in England in the summer. But we can buy them in the shops almost all year round because many fruit and vegetables are brought from other countries to sell here.

All the food in this shop was grown in England.

Most fruit and vegetables were not rationed either during or just after the war, but there were often shortages. Many people grew fruit and vegetables in their own gardens.

I remember...

Frank Fenton can still remember the first time he saw a banana. 'My friend, Sid, brought a banana in to school to show us. His dad had got it from a mate. Sid gave me a bite. I thought it was amazing. It wasn't like anything I'd ever eaten before.'

The Fentons are using a pedestrian crossing to cross the road.

The High Street is very busy. There are cars, taxis and buses. Sometimes there are traffic jams, especially when lorries unload goods outside shops.

It was easy to cross the road in this High Street.

Fifty years ago, there were not as many cars on the road as there are today. This meant that even the High Street was usually free from traffic jams.

I remember...

Sally Fenton used to go into town with her mum on Saturdays. 'I loved walking down the High Street, looking in the shop windows. Every week there seemed to be more things coming into the shops. Every few shops my mum would stop and say, "Well, I haven't seen one of those since before the war!"

It became quite a joke.'

NOTES FOR PARENTS

This book is designed to be used on many different levels.

The words in bold provide a simple, core text. The rest of the text provides greater detail, more background information and some personal reminiscences. Competent readers will be able to tackle the entire text themselves. Younger readers could share the reading of the text with an adult. Non-readers will benefit from hearing the text read aloud to them.

All children will enjoy comparing and contrasting the main pictures on each double-page spread. Every picture is a rich resource with much that can be observed and discussed. Ideas for discussion points and questions to ask about each photograph can be found below.

Children are likely to have relatives who will have clear memories of everyday life fifty years ago. There is nothing that brings history to life more vividly than personal recollections. If these memories can be supported by photographs or other artefacts, such as things that may have been bought at that time, then the experience is made all the more 'real' to a child.

This particular book is about the high street. Fifty years ago, many goods were still rationed. Children could think about how this affected everyday life. They could consider the similarities and differences between the high street today and fifty years ago. In many instances, the types of business, such as banks and toy shops, have remained the same, but advances in technology have made significant changes, to both the types of goods that are in the shops and the way they are purchased.

About the Photographs

Toy shop p 5

Questions to ask:
Which toys look similar to toys you might find today?
Which look different?

Points to explore:
Ask friends and relatives about the toys they used to play with fifty years ago.
Think about how advances in technology have changed toys, e.g. computerized toys and radio-controlled toys.

Barber p 7

Questions to ask:
What is the barber wearing over his ordinary clothes?
What do you think of the young man's hairstyle?

Points to explore:
Try to find some photographs of your friends and relatives fifty years ago and look at their hairstyles.
Compare the hair-styles with today's styles.

Bank p 9

Questions to ask:
What can you see between the bank clerk and the customer?
What would be there today?

Points to explore:
Think about how computers have changed the way we pay for things, e.g. credit cards and charge cards.
Talk about 'old' money and try to find some examples.

Butcher p 11

Questions to ask:
Where did the butcher chop the meat?
What sort of things did he sell?

Points to explore:
Find out what rationing was and how long it lasted.
Try to find some recipes from fifty years ago.

Clothes shop p 13

Questions to ask:
What sort of clothes are the women in this photograph wearing?
What is different from today's styles?

Points to explore:
Find out what was fashionable for men fifty years ago.
Try to find a picture of someone wearing a New Look dress.

Baker p 15

Questions to ask:
What types of cake can you see? What else was sold in this shop, besides cakes and bread?

Points to explore:
See if your friends and relatives have any memories of their local baker's shop.
Find out how much a loaf of bread cost fifty years ago.

Post Office p 17

Questions to ask:
What is the man behind the screen wearing?
What is on the counter next to him?

Points to explore:
Find out about differences in the way that mail is sorted today compared with fifty years ago.
Try to find some stamps from fifty years ago.

Library p 19

Questions to ask:
How many children can you see in this picture?
Can you describe what they are doing?

Points to explore:
Ask friends and relatives what their favourite books used to be. Find out how they were expected to behave in their local library.

Supermarket p 21

Questions to ask:
Can you describe what the woman in the picture is wearing? As well as a description of the goods and a price, what else can you see on the shelf labels?

Points to explore:
Find out more about the points system, which was a type of food rationing.
Discover what 'blue peas' and 'groats' are.

Cafe p 23

Questions to ask:
How would you describe this cafe?
What is the waitress wearing?

Points to explore:
Discover more information about Lyons' Corner Houses.
Find out about 'British Restaurants', which were opened during the war after bombs damaged many restaurants.

Greengrocer p 25

Questions to ask:
What is on the shelf behind the shopkeeper and the customer? What is the shopkeeper using to put vegetables in the woman's bag?

Points to explore:
Compare the types of fruit and vegetables available today and fifty years ago. Talk about people growing fruit and vegetables in gardens and allotments.

The High Street p 27

Questions to ask:
How many cars can you see? Do you think this picture was taken in summer or winter?

Points to explore:
Find out about other high street shops fifty years ago, e.g. chemists and sweetshops.
Find out how shoppers travelled to the high street.

GLOSSARY

 **balance** A set of scales that measures the weight of something.

 **barber** A barber is a men's hairdresser. Fifty years ago, barbers' shops often had a red and white striped pole outside.

 **New Look** A style of women's clothes which was the idea of a famous French fashion designer called Christian Dior.

 **penny** There were 12 pennies in a shilling and 240 pennies in a pound. An old penny was worth less than half of 1p.

 **phone box** You can still see old-fashioned red telephone boxes in some places. The phones had dials instead of buttons for the numbers.

 **pound** This is a pound note. A pound was made up of 20 shillings. Today we have pound coins.

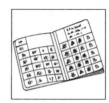 **ration book** Ration books were full of coupons, a bit like stamps. You gave them to the shopkeeper when you bought something that was in short supply.

 **shilling** This coin was worth a shilling. There were 20 shillings in a pound, so a shilling was the same as 5p.

 **telegram** Special messages printed on strips of paper, stuck on to a larger piece of paper and delivered by messenger to a person's house.

 **Utility clothes** This is an example of the Utility style. It was very plain and used as little material as possible.

FURTHER INFORMATION

Books to read

In the Street by K. Bryant-Mole (Wayland, 1994)

In the Street by G. Tanner and T. Wood (A&C Black, 1995)

People in the Town by K. Bryant-Mole (Wayland, 1996)

Shopping by G. Tanner and T. Wood (Black, 1993)

Shopping for Food by Ruth Thomson (Watts, 1992)

Shopkeepers Worldwide by J. Shuter (Heinemann, 1997)

Use this book for teaching literacy

This book can help you in the literacy hour in the following ways:

✓ By extending the skills of reading non-fiction. There are two levels of text given, a simple version and a more advanced level.

✓ By encouraging children to articulate and then try to answer questions provoked by the pictures.

✓ They can be encouraged to ask relatives about their lives as children and learn about history through personal experiences.

✓ They can write stories about what their lives would have been like fifty years ago.

INDEX